On Shaving Off His Face

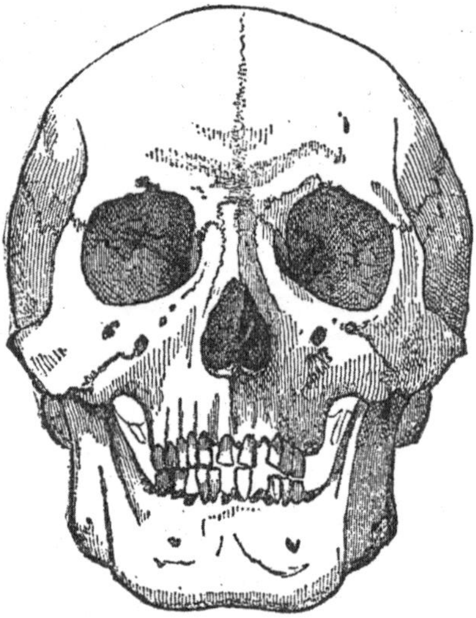

ON SHAVING OFF HIS FACE

POEMS

SHANE NEILSON

The Porcupine's Quill

Library and Archives Canada Cataloguing in Publication

Neilson, Shane, 1975–, author
On shaving off his face : poems / Shane Neilson.

ISBN 978-0-88984-382-0 (paperback)

I. Title.

PS8577.E33735057 2015 C811'.6 C2015-902259-2

1 2 3 • 17 16 15

Published by The Porcupine's Quill, 68 Main Street, PO Box 160, Erin, Ontario NOB ITO. http://porcupinesquill.ca

Edited for the press by Jim Johnstone.

Represented in Canada by Canadian Manda Group.
Trade orders are available from University of Toronto Press.

We acknowledge the support of the Ontario Arts Council and the Canada Council for the Arts for our publishing program. The financial support of the Government of Canada through the Canada Book Fund is also gratefully acknowledged.

Canada Council for the Arts / Conseil des Arts du Canada

Canada

ONTARIO ARTS COUNCIL
CONSEIL DES ARTS DE L'ONTARIO
an Ontario government agency
un organisme du gouvernement de l'Ontario

Ontario
Ontario Media Development Corporation

… one
Staggers into the bathroom and stares in the glass
To meet one's madness …

W.H. Auden

[O]

(For all the faces in mourning)

For Zee

For Kaz

Table of Contents

ON SHAVING OFF HIS FACE

BOOK ONE

If I could stand off from myself
In a thoughtful haze called the soul of the world
And watch myself without myself being aware,
Not every motion flatteringly studied and rehearsed as it is in a mirror,
I might not even like myself or actually be too awed
For like or dislike: but then the razor and its blade
Are also poised, also studied—reflected in the mirror.

Milton Acorn, 'On Shaving Off His Beard'

1. General Preamble

They looked and knew what was wrong. Your face designed to break and break again on illness. Blood and alcohol the rural isolate you wear as helmet. But skin-masks envelop grief-masks. More blood, alcohol, and always *need*. Your face immerses except for wonder, baptismal fonts troubled by your father with the face of icon, who presses his own face to an oilrag and transfers to you his terrible sainthood. The Saint of Fear: Nicholas of Myra.

You learn a rictus grin for all goodnights to chasten the tongues that chide teeth, a sound that mimics the closing of gates. Blame is the function of your face. You are here, wanderer, to be known by how you come. If we welcome you, it is because we take your face and emblazon our flags against your cause, a cause so plainly seen. To be free! But you cannot be, for your face is pain's currency. Others spend it for you.

Not proud, nor revenant of the self, a woman taught you first and best that dreams of death are madly coming true, squandered is the dream.

Look at yourself and know that the common went predictably wrong on some beginning ago. A line to comprise a face: *the fire was want*. But it's not true. Fire melts a face and makes it into what fire wants: the reformation of burn.

You are free to yearn as your face coils, recoils, falls, and resurrects. Look one last time. Take the oilrag. Press it there.

2. No Sum

There is no such thing as a sum of suffering, for no one suffers it.
C.S. Lewis

The face is the sum, the host, the wreck,
the face is a holocaust, holodomor, a novel mass death,
the nuclear face immolates tongue-licked suns,
the face a disguise of one man, one.

3. Facial Structure

The grief of what's been gotten past, surpassed, a love supreme!

(the next time)

and yea the offence, yea the defence, yea though you walk through broken streets kissing the drowned and the saved, the wounded and the depraved, the brave and the impossibly free;

(the next time)

sick with the idea that people can live as the sun wraps past a hundred thousand spires:

4. St. Anthony's Fire

alights. Imagine Christ rye-laden, his gangrenous fingers full of blessings, the witches of Salem dancing in the fields, the ergot lysergic constricting throats and vessels and sanity, filibustering the guts and men asking *why*, the monks of St. Anthony with the perfect cure: all things in abstinence, attention placed on doomed limbs and poultices applied to god in your image. Robbed of touch with peripheral neuropathies and visible sores, the manna from heaven contaminated with *Claviceps purpurea*, whole civilizations monster-movied, disease being the measure of purity in a lost heaven, break bread with them, O lord, break bread with them and have them hallucinate you, have them taste the manic essence of *Ignis Sacer*, have them wither and waver and tuck their too-suffering children in at night, quivering in the fear of all unknown, this ingested pestilence, this rictus gift. The truth: your curses are the miracles we know first.

5. The Graph

Outlier: check the graph, see the trace.
The face trending downward, the place
you came from, quantified: when love
was replaced with an opening quality,
a black line routing up. Your children's faces:
pre-sorrow, your view before the heart
made due. They look to you:
you hold them as the only sentence of grace,
the only kind you're given to know.
The graph is your arms, reaching round,
lifting them up, and you swear you're free.
You can't be.

6. St. Vitus' Dance

A jig. Pray to god and little basal ganglia bugs that stand at attention and command *March.* Your face flails according to order: *choreathetoid, choreathetoid*, your jerky-sinuous lips pulled and pushed to command the martial music of a possessed two-year-old who can't sleep because his heart bugs have autoimmuned. *Sleep, Child* a mother says, and the great Sydenham asks *what's in a name* and the febrile child is coursing, his mother applies cold cloths to the forehead, but the child hits invisible targets. Group A *Streptococcus* insists on mad ballet, of buck-sinister crump, the waking hours of the child devoted to marionette tugs. Yet the prognosis is good, the gyrating at St. Vitus' altar proves transient. Look at the child, the body racked, the face ticked, the parents afflicted, praying to patrons.

7. Reaching the Palace

No sign of life, clinical love: pain maidens
scour the walls, leaving no before or clue to after,
only a palliative binge. No visitors! Half-fright,
half-dead, this is the sickroom
where nerves fire, crying wolf
to a brain-hag. You stand at attention every time.

In love with allodynia, abraded connection
and false flag, O signalman, bury you release!
Throes: racked. Wrecked. Wrought
with blunted thought and the kind of ascension
meant for martyrs dying on the cross.
This is loss? Loss is the exact naming of things,
pain's manse and pain's program
and you, suffused, ramshackle and beaten-down,
possess no threshold except the bridal one
when pain steps across the gap
as summons and takes you away, very far away.

8. Facies Leonina

Insensate face of a diseased lion, roaring inward past a smashed nose and pursed, dried lips. Cheek-recession, expanded brow, pockmarks and open sores: what's missing is a florid mane that bathes the face with power, leaving withdrawal perfectly framed. See the snapping maw! Jaws of death, acid-fast dousing the face. Mycobacterium lepræ teems on the head of a pin: here angels dance, slaying the regal slough.

9. Action Potential

The toll road: one unblinking avenue,
hard-wired, forging ahead and licking wounds.
Laugh, calcified. You feel this as you feel
with a heart meant,
with a face meant,
for saying it will all go away:
the hurt, here.

10. Elegy Skyward

Death turns water to flame, your stance hunched and weary of our lady perpetual. One cannot amputate the heart, it is the beating actual. The conclusion is loss, but you do the losing. Open your stiff mouth. Your elegy is a look skyward,

red,

and at the ground,

red.

Not someone in love. No talk of cause. Take a deep breath, a need in the end, hearts are

red,

a man among men.

11. Half-True Incarnations of an About-Face

i. Tiredness begets error. You erred by not making mistakes last, but first. You cannot summon maths to calculate.

ii. Covered in shit, vomit, and urine: your harangue to the floor. How did you get here? You, half in love and half in anger with the dialectics of the real fall: away, always, and near. Raving, rousing, roughhousing, allegiance to the sharp, unpredictable turn: your answers are entirely your own.

iii. You deny these things because they are meant for men, and you consider yourself a cause.

iv. Borne are gifts that make you stronger. Paranoia inverts into sense: fall through copper memories until fists burnish the tarnish with want. Buried are your dreams under years of deluge from your mouth, nose, eyes, and ears. These red features are maimed seers on an indivisible target.

v. Elision: cerebellum antsy until it's lying flat. You drank to win the whiskey-whetted keys to the kingdom. Indecipherable ciphers from before, you grasped *after*.

vi. Your face the better angel, though you cursed it for what you needed to know. Archangel paranoia blessed you in the middle of the worst, compelled to go but never to stay, lost here.

Women touched in the night don't understand.

Madness as circuitbreaker, jawbreaker, liar and lorn: in errands of anger you bled and heard plots in your ear like a cathedral choir. You were led here, to the grime and the dust. You were led to last rites with no calculation of cost: your face not unbroken

but lashed to the lost.

Mad. Their word. Yours: free, the curse you cut your teeth with.

vii. Your face a firefighter entering a burning building, a fire-eater swallowing gasoline, a Hindenburg erupting against the sky. She touched your face and felt the pressing why, the need of space filling immolated distances, the urge to erase fire. Were you beautiful? Remember yourself as an effigy to burn and forget.

Burnt offerings of love and anger to a vanquished god. She gathered up your cause, a flag-bearer for ends, in love with ends and the prophet of beaten precincts. Hear the vatic muttering, the stalled shouts, her beautiful.

viii. The weary come to call out their dead, eyes slack and drifting, faces flat and listing. All love points away. Your expression was its barest chance.

Face blunted and dull, mistaken and mistook: a drenched dry well, troubled by leavings. Once lost, he became a gallows, a subsumed rictus, a folding bet. You held up a semblance for all to regret. Darkroomed cloister, see that you still choose: take down the barrier. Make an about-face.

You can't. Head slanted to the left, mouth a chasm, summerteeth, oily hair plated on, there is humour: of agitated eyes that do their holding with a carpenter's hands. Broad nose bloodied a thousand times, love and anger in plaid. See fortune's malfeasance in years worn on the jaw, but a man used to shaving: clean-cut in opposition, the thrum of capture and open-neck a straight shot to rolled-up sleeves. A deep-seated grin jury-rigged to diametric dialectics. Your face threw itself into the camera, all it has, open and unremonstrated, contradictions resolved there.

ix. Illness seconded, is seeing things, is hearing things. Hear your witnesses recount when they are sure they have seen and heard a thing when you are no longer sure of your own senses except to remember that no wonder is mistake. You heard no witness tend to you, they tended the targets in your brain.

x. Every man stands on the precipice that precedes him. O little love, a half-true half-incarnation, I watched you to see how it is done.

xi. The tumult wed leaves on dying trees, the smoke of signal fires. Once sown, trouble grew into menacing, beautiful flowers. To anecdotes, to assemblage, to the sadness-bound. The place of the dead, crazy scaffolds, no thought of torches, cause, or even home, a wayfarers' last step only, the grand whim spent. Lie in stasis: life not lived as cause, but as *for* or *against*.

As if you were undertaker of the age—

xii. Force: up from within, the found and the rent, voice hoarse and blood tuned, the vessels your vassals, your face red. Force: the elements held in the clenched hand. Who could defy your grief musculature?

xiii. With sense abandoned, fire abandons its clansman, fuel. You leaked light for years. No fire warms what's dead.

xiv. Would you go back and change the debts, dues, and the goddamned? Your head always turned according to the direction you were in. Across, across, you call—and the loss isn't here.

xv. Power coursing at opposites: a crucifix that lifts up the afflicted a few terrible feet. But the cause, the cause, however brief.

xvi. The land of rancour, the afterland of need where you are still needed, baring secrets. Fool poets who call the spring green: sad friend, you cannot change.

12. The Pain Face

Rigid, stoic, mask: broken-bone face,
gunshot face, son-dead face.

Look, the face: see your rictus
fortune in icterus, the yellow glow

on a one-to-ten scale. Consider the Pain Face:
love on your lip, love sliding sideways

to make a silly face of pre- and post.
Profess systems of belief, of research:

corollary, corollary, sing. Agreeably sing
of pain as shadow cast by this edifice:

the love face.

Pain's place is pictorial, a hundred thousand
atlases of your face: tear-stained, unfathomed

by intense algorithms of validated claims.
See the Pain Face. Underneath it is no face.

13. Face-Shaver

No appearances whatever are infallible proofs of grace.
William James

In my face is proof of life and death, no masks but these.
Look close to see eternities of axe and dove. Grace emitted
in grimaces given to those who know I'm off, wrong,
embattled by stars. Counterbalance: get the fuck away.
I sleep with a jaw writhed by dreams, acting out funny faces as I flee
from Face-Shaver who waves his visage-bag, saying: let's say grace
together. Then I wake into days that balance on the vermilion border,
up-lip, down-lip, or the ragged crease in between, God roaring in freedom
and shedding light to witness the fount. Look at my face:
asymmetric not-rights coalescing into view.

I'm either you in the mirror or in the Face-Shaver's blade.
Face-Shaver says infallible proofs are graven images.
The grave left to grass, abiding epitaphs,
the graceful plots, the presaging stones.
Either you did it or you didn't do it, so say this with me:
grace is condemned to leave us alone.

14. They, to!

Anger to alone and beaten they better it bleeding will die than edge they far is free men grave far hallowed before in wrested idea weren't learning would last trace mammals their on stood purpose suspend.

15. Little Lethals of Music

Across a divide that spills and spills
into wills, deeds, and your face,
your heart. Estrangement
locks bullets into four chambers,
love an endothermic curse.

Forget this. Forget the song that set
hearts afire, the little lethals of music.
Hear this null instead: is this alive enough,
to wake and feel pain reduce?

16. A Tower for Every Babylon

The house has a thin black line for a roof. Windows shine like the name of god in vain, or a vain god, windows as curses and commandments.

Stick figure on the railing, a red line stretching to blank ground.

Somewhere inside the painting, the artist rests on a recessed bed. On a balcony, the flight of a child begins, unseen.

A line streaks into the sky

to different belief. Raw features, stubble gleaming like a shield, you make the brilliant climb to a courtyard with scorched walls and towers for every faith, towers for every Babel, towers for every Babylon. Stations of the cross come in columns. Meek and bleeding, you profess a colloquial faith in pain. Sorrow straps to wood, two bars strap to your back

in a blasted parsonage on a worthless hillside where dumb shacks hold bitter wives and slaves. Diocletian had a bad idea. This is the way and the lighthouse for etiolated angels who debate graven images, graves, and waiting women. The chapel beaten down to rock, upon the rock a wooden church

standing on a cliff— a sheer drop to the sea. The church falls into the sea. The church is rebuilt on the third day. A local carpenter scavenges shipwrecks and refashions the house of god. The crucifix is formed from two masts broken in a storm. The carpenter hammers nails in the son and holy ghost positions. The carpenter is also a priest, the priest of this church. When it is time to push the church into the sea, you take confession and put your hands again to the wood, feel the nail rusted by holy water. Now a different day, a day when you entered the wood church, the day when you were born. Believers carried alms and torches. You watched them break knees open on the marble floors, saw their dead carried on shoulders, and heard heavenly choirs. You remember a priest who remade you as new. How many churches since, churches of gold and silver where master artisans spent a year on Christ's agonized hands, hands directing you to a cast-out kingdom

through the north gate where mothers and fathers are announced by stones. Sedate a lamb for a child. Gather lambs, petrify them, affix them to tombs! Gather lambs as if they are your own children. In holding them you hold a shovel, you're wide-eyed and digging the tombs of little lambs— flee after witnessing a fifty-flock, then scuttle back through the north gate. Focus on two graves, lambs you've long sacrificed on a faulty altar, some wrong ritual you carry like tablets, god-inscribed, only to throw down at the feet of the more afflicted! Those epitaphs are names in vain. Your name is your face.

17. The Lake of Fire

When the burn came, the skin became armour.
Tombstones and churches,
spires and the holy statues. *Harden.*

Emerge into white, your skin black,
intention a mercenary.

Face the crusade and take your blade
to cut the throat of what you want:
deenervated skin that degloves with the touch
of anything but steel.

Sleep and leave a hole.

Nobody see me you say, hands over your eyes. Then you see.
Another golden wall. A mirror, a wanton trooper,
the right hand and the left hand cleaving goldenrod.
In him, with him. Ever the downy air, each weave a holy handiwork:
leave them as you shall leave?

18. No Sky

You, when the last were first.
At the last, at last.
You waited.
Dove sounds, sky choirs, repentant desert thirst.

If you die before you wake,
what kind of promise to make?

The promise of childhood, when skies open
as the earth opens, when horizons yawn and burn, is this your fate?

Up above the sky so high, you make this final wish a lie:
you will be—flesh of your flesh?

No—the sky.

ABLE PHYSIOLOGISTS

BOOK TWO

DISCUSS GRIEF MUSCULATURES

I stopped going to the conferences because most of us are all gone.

William Patterson

Conference Preamble: Fervourism

(A theory presented by Charles Darwin, excerpted from a larger work entitled *The Expression of Emotions in Man and Animals.*)

From its importance, our present subject must be discussed at some little length; and it is always advisable to perceive clearly our ignorance. It is impossible to decide how much weight ought to be attributed to our Theory of Fervourism. The insane are studied, as they are liable to the strongest passions, and give uncontrolled vent to them.

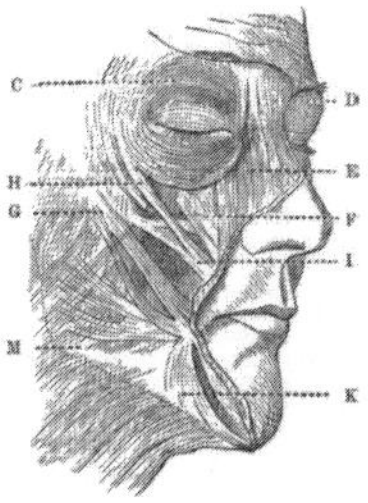

When the sensorium is strongly excited, nerve-force is generated in excess, and is transmitted in certain definite directions, depending on the connection of the nerve-cells, and partly on habit. The least excitement of a sensitive nerve does react on the heart, even when a nerve is touched so slightly that no pain can possibly be felt. Hence when the mind is strongly excited, we might expect that it would instantly affect in a direct manner the heart; and this is universally acknowledged and felt to be the case.

Expressions serve to gratify some desire or relieve a sensation. If often repeated, the expressions become so habitual that they are performed, whether or not of any service, whenever the same desire or sensation is felt, even in a very weak degree.

Only a few expressive movements are learnt by each individual; the far greater number of the movements of expression, and all the more important ones, are innate or inherited. We know that the vaso-motor system, which regulates the capillary circulation, is much influenced by the mind.

Fear again is the most depressing of all the emotions, as if in consequence of the most violent and prolonged attempts to escape from the danger, though no such attempts have actually been made. The internal consciousness that is the nervous system strengthens, though in a subordinate degree, the tendency to violent action under extreme suffering.

The head being raised, with erected ears and eyes directed forwards, gives an unmistakable expression of close attention to any animal. The insane notoriously give way to all their emotions with little or no restraint. Patients suffering from acute fear have paroxysms of blubbering in the midst of their incoherent ravings.

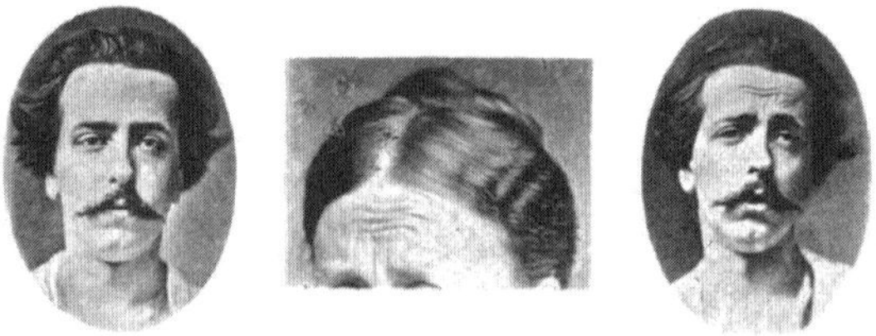

Frowning, which is one of the most important of all the expressions in man, is due to the contraction of the corrugators. The circulation becomes languid; the face pale; the muscles flaccid; the head hangs on the contracted chest; the lips, cheeks, and lower jaw all sink downwards from their own weight. Hence all the features are lengthened; and the face of a person who hears bad news is said to *fall*. With respect to the eyebrows, they assume an oblique position owing to the contraction of the orbiculars, corrugators, and pyramidals of the nose, which together tend to lower and contract the eyebrows. The contraction of the more powerful central fasciæ raise the inner ends of the eyebrows; and as the corrugators at the same time draw the eyebrows together, their inner ends become puckered into a fold or lump. The eyebrows are at the same time somewhat roughened, owing to the hairs being made to project.

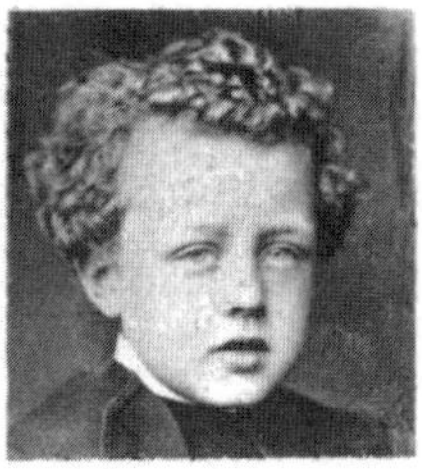

All these aforementioned muscles, when thus in conjoint yet opposed action, may be called, for the sake of brevity, the grief-muscles.

The above actions may be considered as rudimentary vestiges of the screaming-fits, which are frequent and prolonged during infancy. Few persons, without some practice, can voluntarily act on their grief-muscles; but after repeated trials a considerable number succeed whilst others never can. Yet in all cases of distress, whether great or small, our brains tend through long habit to send an order to certain muscles to contract, as if we were still infants on the point of screaming out; but this order we, by the wondrous power of the will, are able partially to counteract; although this is effected unconsciously.

Suffering, if great, will from the first have caused screams or groans to be uttered, the body to be contorted, and the teeth to be ground together. Our early progenitors, when suffering from grief or anxiety, would not have made their eyebrows oblique, or have drawn down the corners of their mouth, until they had acquired the habit of endeavouring to restrain their screams. The expression, therefore, of grief and anxiety is *eminently human*.

The movements of expression give vividness and energy to our spoken words. They reveal the thoughts and intentions more truly than do words, which may be falsified. The free expression of an emotion intensifies it. On the other hand, the repression of all outward signs softens our emotions. He who gives way to violent gestures will increase his rage; he who does not control the signs of fear will experience fear in a greater degree; and he who remains passive when overwhelmed with grief loses his best chance of recovering elasticity of mind.

We conclude that the philosophy of our subject has well deserved the attention which it has already received from several excellent observers, and that it deserves still further attention, especially from any able physiologist.

The Conference Begins …

(With an Unfinished Prayer, Followed by a Moment of Silence.)

Saint Lawrence made his own communion each night, drinking the last supper cup filled with holy grog that brought blood from his guts.

The true wealth of the church: the red from reddened mouths. I sit in a small tent underneath heat lightning and Perseid flash, unfinished mistakes on my face.

See gradations of sepulchral devotion, face as holy book burnt for warmth. For too long I've mistook beauty for grace. But grace is a hand's breadth from my face.

See the motion of the tent's blue membrane, soon to be soaked and battered by wind on the increase. Is this prayer or just another layer separating elements that authenticate?

I want to be away from this sit, stare, and witness-bear to a bird's-egg wall that shoves grace closer. Answer to my prayers: *feeling authenticates nothing you've done.*

Stagnant water down the hill erects a stage for choked green and a mass of winged black. What the hell, better accounts exist of flickering heaven:

consider medieval artists who rendered the death of saints with paint, martyrs erupting from mouths of men as hellish fire. We go to god through flame.

I take love and call it by that other name, wonder. What is past the tent wall?

I rescind all knowledge of beauty. To chase the beautiful is to be outpaced by beauty every time. All my heroes are dead because of the draft to the cause.

For or against, beauty permits no election. Give me love that proves pleasure is worth its target; sneak beauty past my sense. Graft the word freedom upon our cause.

Only then I'll fight for what I thought I wanted, thinking the fight entirely beautiful: strange men, estranged women, comfort that comes when comfort is seized.

Yet I bleed on the earth and have never found release. I cannot be convinced; you don't care anyway. I never fought for an alibi irrigated with blood.

Heroes refuse the role. Up the path is a red and yellow shack with books, desk, and a bed for an absent man who has all night to watch the star-shot heavens relegate his brain

to targets. Pilgrims to this site go to bed in the heat and wake up in the cold. With a weak flashlight I succumbed and walked into the shack. I saw a paper Acorn on the wall, his baffled, sloughed face veering past a shoulder that turns to an unfinished stone

monument. O Sam Lount and Peter Matthews, what prayer is this again? Whose?

Should I have saluted the crow face on the wall? Back in the tent the wind picked a blue wall to buckle; recursive stars disappeared, cursed to return.

The Perseids fought the clouds. Beauty is never free. It is costly built and demands an unfinished price. I opened the flap and asked out loud, 'Whose prayer?'

I slept an hour. The best causes are not projected upon triumphant skies. I've tasted my blood enough to know blood refuses ceremony. Blood sits as still as the brackish river

down the hill. Saint Lawrence, your martyrdom was fierce, you were burnt to be killed, just as you are burnt in return to sleep again. Let us begin with curses and silence.

Let us pray.

An Able Physiologist 1

(Phillipe Pinel and the Wisdom of the Clinical.)

L'introduction de Nosographie philosophique, ou La méthode de l'analyse appliquée à la médecine

A father, yes. Passions in men extend. The revolution is not
our true parent. At the Helvétius salon in Paris, I cast my lot
with the set behaviours of murderers. My revolutionary thought
was: not everyone is mad, even madmen. Wholesale, I bought
the moral to my therapy: eat, drink, and emote the revolution of self.
In Bicêtre I transcribed the natural history of natural causes.
The natural state of man is chains.

A good friend died once from his nature—I too am inward.
He needed talk, his head presaging the realm of the dead.
I reject the concept that he no longer wanted his warm bed,
wife, and acclaim. I knew him like I know myself. The moral
to his unsought therapy is: love well, and love the chains.
My life is dedicated to his self-bereavement. He died
not far from here. I ask: what is lack? In the guillotine gleam,
thousands of patients have taught me the natural admixture
of desire and fear, the dumb look that comes after the loss of
their heads. And before:

Cause 1: chagrin d'amour

Men compose endless letters—yet their passionate pitch estranges love.
The lover may be unsuitable but men *need.*
Such creatures stalk Bicêtre and lapse into monologues.
I interrupt to ask, 'Where are you?' Then I point to a painting
of the asylum by a former patient. Most of us suffer this derangement
at least once in our lives but these afflicted fail to adjust to being alone.

Cause 2: deuil national

The illness of a child is an illness of love. If the child dies,
men may choose to grieve through god
to find a sudden affidavit: a father wakes in an asylum.

Cause 3: extase religieuse

Men wish to be Jesus because of the son of God's orgiastic suffering.
The stigmata phenomenon I have witnessed myself.
These men have the worst prognosis because they wish to be loved.
Love fails—this is our natural state and inescapable chain.
Men resort to a physiologic sympathy: the poor miracle of blood,
a blade slicing through a membrane, their hands palm-out
in fervent glee as if to say, 'God has chosen me.' I can only agree,
then point to the painting.

Cause 4: événements de la Révolution

Public events influence the emotions. In Paris, events sharpen
the self according to the revolution's guillotine gifts.
When women die as spectacle and warning, the execution crowd is affected.
One case: post-revolution, my barber became obsessed with the guillotine.
He believed his head had been severed and reattached to the wrong body.
What's wrong with your body? I said to his head.
Then I asked his body: *What's wrong with your head?*
Self-dialectic: he was cured.

Cause 5: excès de ferveur patriotique

External passion for what? Love this land as what, and for what?
I tell men they love France as their own selves.
France's abilities and might, France's glorious history,
France must defeat her enemies! The virtue of France! Her honour!
Spittle! Feculent breath! I ask these men if they know how to be better citizens,
then I house them near true cast-offs of the republic, the poor.
As a doctor I do no more than my former patient's solemn
picture of Bicêtre: I paint truth as exterior.

An Able Physiologist 2

(Benjamin Rush Sings 'Battle Hymn of the Republic'.)

The mad in the asylum all sing their Christian songs.
Admitted with good riddance, some rave the whole night long,
and when the morning comes I find that God's left them alone.
I sift out hearts of men.

(chorus)

Their songs seem true enough that I wonder if I'm wrong,
if therapy and charity can switch into unknowns.
But on the earth are faces ruined by what cannot be shown.
God is marching on.

(chorus)

A method to their madness and a method to my care,
I appeal to the man behind each incurable stare,
if love can be diminished, I take satisfaction there
and steal from God in fear.

(chorus)

Founders of this republic were wary of within,
how men go mad from passion and guillotine their kin.
They knew that freedom easily subjugates to sin,
that freedom has a sting.

(chorus)

But man inside can suffer odds he can never win,
turned against his nature he can't turn back again.
Accommodating less is what splits the mad from men.
Also means and ends.

(chorus)

Most of my patients are the abandoned poor
the republic couldn't sponsor except to make some more,
every franc requires a closed door—
what asylums underscore.

(chorus)

The men in the asylum forget their reasons why
they cannot live with truth or with a better lie,
they look at me for answers and I do not even try.
Better to live than to die?

Chorus:

Glory glory to the ill,
glory glory to angels,
glory glory to the killed,
the truth will shill and fail.

An Able Physiologist 3

(Robin Pecknold Descends the Steps of Pennsylvania Hospital in 1786.)

... [t]he only foundation for a useful education in a republic is to be laid in Religion. Without this there can be no virtue, and without virtue there can be no liberty, and liberty is the object and life of all republican governments.

Benjamin Rush

Always down. On the marbled steps I refuse to sing like the bird
held in the cage it flew into, or made. I look back at the hospital:
how long it was, a thousand years before, I came and beat my breast
against bars erected to keep me safe, bars that predicted my arrival
based on oncoming song. The doctor here mentioned the moon,
used leeches and cups, forbade me to sing. Was my difficulty a woman?
Sexual inanition? I can't remember, though I feel the same.
All I hoped would change within me stayed. The breaks occur
along faults that crack when no pressure is applied.

I am not mad. It was a woman. She held me as a delusion does,
seeking out weaknesses—in the morning the sufferer wakes up
enlightened and without distraction. I wandered the town for a week
afraid to think or see and sung folk hymns to God.

The doctor suggests impiety is my problem. I told him I never believed
and never would. He asked why I knew the words to the hymns.
I said I wanted to believe that the holy spirit is a bird cloistered
in church attics, refused flight, kept in the dark. We all hear the bird
trying to escape. And so I know the words, melody, and beat
to the praiseful songs. Still the doctor would not let me sing,
allowed no visitors either: *too fragile a case*, quiet and dark
my prescribed treatments.

To stay alive I dreamed of birds
keeping a moonlit exile on Lake Erie,
no man or god troubling these mute,
unheard birds who exist in me. I turn now,
the brittle steps enclosed in a canopy
of green, the sun so rarely seen in my stay
beating down upon all it hits and flattens
and makes better, all love turning towards
the great light to disintegrate. A bird that sings
or a bird that has no song: after all is said
and after all is done, God only knows which of them
I'll become.

An Able Physiologist 4

(In the tongue of schizophasics,
Emil Kræpelin argues nightly for sexual hygiene.)

My own dreams interpret the dreamer.
No word is a strange dream, too common are my words
to make sense of shouts, mutterings, and associations?

Yes,

once I dreamed I was in a room with Ina, my sleeping wife. I stood and said to the self-stunned dreamer, 'What interest dreams, if dreams are biological?' This question took me fifty dreamed years on a night when my wife classified our lives as unhappy, restricting me to never touch her again. We had four daughters together. That night made the last entry in a personal record of three hundred dreams:

dream record 300

Love the undergird and purloined loin,
love absurd in a coordinal red breast
and cardinal, love the racked black
brow and bow and bough, love in Trieste's
bloodflows and arrows and never any shields,
love without women and men and never
any shields, love condemned in buildings
and undergirded in construction,
love of loins and love of listening in,
the transcribed love of what is in me,

in lava and category and error
and chorion and amnion and sorrow-ward
and roam, love the mistake made when young,
the substitute placeholder and alternate song,
the bell rung as men and women are hung
arm in arm in me in front of me and behind me
and in me in love without love in me
and the meme of me and do this in memory of me
and Luther reformed the me in me and the poor heart,
never any shield.

An Able Physiologist 5

(Lead Belly Serenades Baptisms in the Holy Spirit,
Two Performances.)

1.

Take a great notion of Saturdays and morphine
and reduce it to a river scene, Irene and I
at play amidst a minstrel. The song sings
of goodnight and ways of parting; I begged
her not to go, I begged her, but she felt
the trees and the water were like my sick soul.
She left singing a lyric about drowning
that had long been my own thought,
to return to my wife and family with no breath
and the knives of Texarkana in my neck
and the underaged of Louisiana saddled with seed
and all the things I'd never touched (not even my face)
or did but kept bitter and close to my wife and family
who bid *return, return*. All of these dreams
reduce to a river, Irene led me there and baptised me
with promises of ghosts and fire. She left.
I fell into a great and deep notion that I would dream her dry.

2.

And I went down to the river to pray, never knowing another way,
baptised my feet in a font of stones, O lord, let me drown. O lord, you
let me drown, you let me go deep and you let me drown, I surfaced with

a dirt robe and a grass crown, I went down to the river to pray. I realized I lost my way, I couldn't find where the choir had gone, but O lord, you showed me the way. On my knees and on my hands, my face in the water and no breath at last, a great draught of river and the Sunday preacher at bay, O lord, I met you today. Men and women laughed in the branches that reach to you, O lord, to show me what's free. O lord, I exchanged a slave's love song for

your starry crown, for split hooves that beat good men down, *you* never felt what I feel now, O lord, it is so sweet to be

so sweet to be rid of me, you let me drown, I sank down yes I wanted to go down, down past where searchers from the town see, O lord, they won't find my body. There is no hell, no baptismal fire, no archangel balancing upon a wire, no band of lovers looking concerned, no constable marking probable paths,

O lord?

My lungs burned as I became heavenly,
this river claimed me at long and at last, the church of the present is built on the rock of the past, John dipped my head and silenced the trees, O lord, you showed me the dream.

An Able Physiologist 6

(The Lost Writings of Clifford Whittingham Beers, composed during involuntary commitment to the New Haven State Asylum, part of a planned manuscript titled *A Mind That Found Itself*, and confiscated by Dr. ______.)

CH. X

A glass shard is enough to cut out a lung, amputate my breath, and make my conservator brother learn that trussed madmen speak in blood. In this place my face is hated by brutes that beat the poor, sick, and unreasoned down with chairs and fists. Attendants choke us, ringing gasped stars. I wish to write of strange flowers seen on accompanied walks taken four months ago. I wish to write of a pummelled man carried in a sheet as if he were a dog led to convalescence.

I am unlike what I had been before, and unlike what I have been since.

Before, in the White Mountains, I tried to improve upon the self and came across a hatred that writes upon walls. My handwriting said: 'At the last, you will praise the Lord.' The writing sprung upon bedsheets, clothes, books, and towels. I ran out the fourth-floor window and met my family eating dinner below. I did not fall unconscious. I felt powdered glass between vertebræ and my legs were useless, broken.

CH. XI

A nurse shaves my legs for the surgeon, the ritual of the shave worse than my pain. I hate paraphernalia more than control's setting to right. The professionals cut with exquisite blades and ether. My legs mend to visions of butterflies and moths an unnaturalist named never, pinks and blues and great greys that splay upon the sheets and walls and reduced room, light refracted through wings into a settled script I see again. Selfish beauty instructs: 'At the last, you will praise the Lord.' I close my eyes and still hear the butterflies. Then a detective affixes ice to my smashed heels to obtain a confession of great and true crimes.

Human vipers, stung souls. My hands constrict in a muff tightened to suck out breath. I am chastened to please god and to confess and to submit. Powers that be render blows to my chest—though it cannot expand. The orderlies' hands are paid eighteen dollars a month. Sometimes the doctor pulls the cord of the muff tighter himself, pleased to see suffocating alarm my face. I become unconscious.

CH. XII

A state of elation that breaks the mind and releases all fetters and chains. I write the governor of the state in this state of elation, the governor who is the *ex officio* head of this institution. I write the asylum superintendent too, both men who know it is unreasonable to treat the weak and incompetent with torturous submission prescriptions. No sleep for me. Instead, tens of thousands of words and stratagems for the delivery of epistles. I will tell the truth about every unkind matter as I am beaten for bragging about my plans to the doctors.

I will never get out of here.

I will fly out of here with a flying machine that will win the Commission of the Louisiana Purchase Exposition Prize for Most Efficient Airship and thereby earn millions through my besting of the force of gravity. I will be philanthropic and reform the state of psychiatry in all the Americas!

The act of writing results in an intoxicating pleasure composed of a mingling of emotions that defies analysis.

I defy analysis for 790 days and resort to routine as calm: the order of food and to bed and to rise and to walk outside and to write or to beg to write and to insist to write and to insult idiots who know only to hurt what they don't comprehend. 790 days to look at the writing in my own hand that infects my bed and my sight and tells me to go back to the hand of god which providently dents my wind-pipe. Stars.

The religious instinct is found in primitive man. I am on the mend. Mend is the real language of men.

The medicals and the functionaries and the fellow defectives beat upon me as a drum to hear their superior sound! I shall write about every one of these beatings, a copy of this book sent especial to Dr. ______, MD (Mentally Defective).

But then the state of the lesser when, with privileges, I walk the grounds of the asylum and wonder about the long metal spike held in a tractor-box. Uncanny admixture of sanity! Small enough to secret inside and when provoked, at the best dramatic moment, I can use it upon my wind-pipe. A simple thrust and the blood would drown my lungs. Left in the open, the groundskeepers are cavalier. Inside, attendants count forks (no knives) at the end of each meal, but out here on the grass I fantasize.

I leave the spike in the box. The detectives with ice watch, always; almost every night my brain is at battledore and shuttlecock with weird thoughts. One night I take out a pencil and write on the walls; it dulls, so I gnaw it to sharpness. Elation masses; the routine of no sleep again, my words on the walls possessed of insolence—

that night I artistically damn all men and barricade the door with my desk, bed, and two books: *Paradise Lost* and the King James Bible. My writing is best. The door is broken down, my neck is throttled, and I am dragged back to confines of other violently touched men.

When they give me paper and lead again, I write a poem of great fluency about light,
and the secrets
of God
and the leaps
of will
and grim knowledge
and realms.

My mind has mended in the language. I find myself in the country of the Gadarenes among tombs where men cannot be chained due to possession, the fetters applied but plucked asunder, neither could any men tame them, and when Jesus came, the tomb-dwellers approached Jesus and said,

'I adjure thee by God, that thou torment us not.'

So beauty instructs, and at the last.

An Able Physiologist 7

(Three Essays Facing One Another.)

i. Adam Lanza Cannot Smash His Face

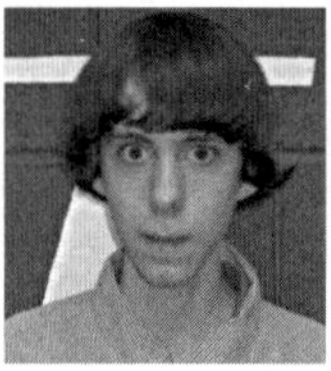

The scapegoat of face as ineradicable as hate.
For all the faces in mourning, the ill are viewed
from a safe distance, in two dimensions.

The killer's static smirk: *we always knew, it could only be you.*

Apocalypse as culture-doubt comes
in waves,
in prison wall searchlight,
in stage spotlight,
in slivers of glass exploded from god

and now rain as reports of the preordained.

The smirk roves across the face like a crack in a shard
and through it we see the chosen evil
and the safe at night
and the blame
and the everlasting why.

We want stories capped by happy endings.
But the happy ending is why people fall
into,
out of
love.
The results kill children in homeroom seats before they learn the capital
cities of states.

O love
it is not hate that I have
or could ever hold
but in my face is a riot of Columbines
that could have been,
every word an aimless death-rattle in the halls.
Who is the saviour of us all?
Is it glass blasted out by Glock deliverance?

Evening faces decline why but advise:
Put a guard at every school,
kill each child as they enter,
catch the kids in the headlights of a black Honda Civic,
snap shy photographs for the school yearbook.

But which one for our news? The face in the glare a composite sketch
of scare
and the there but for the grace of glass
and rain
and not me, but meme.

ii. The Jared Loughner Face Meme

The principal walks in. I have to lean forward and kind of bend to see him. He's maybe five seven, 135 pounds … he isn't smirking or denying math. The word problem: if a killer driving a car at 40 mph is 3.6 miles away, how long before you stop your speech?

The killer's face slides into a smirked pudge of abraded, ventilated skull. Nowadays all faces profess angry health. These exemplary faces command the televisioned choir: we would not, evil lead not us into temptation, delivered by sound mind, our face does not look like that.

Locked up, seen only when we click. Mayhem Fest!!! Look, my eagerlings, into this Leibniz equation:

$\int_{y_0}^{y_1} f(x, y)\, dy$ where x = eat and y = sleep and
the function symbol = brush teeth.

In the valley of gun
the face is gun,
the face on laughing gas,
the dazed spectacle of
the land needing a proof in
the form of a cull,

in columns,
in sums,

be evangelical with the ill who must never, never ever, we sleep in
the valley of gun and wake to gunshots,
the glade is green and
the flood-bathed plain is green and we are tempted in
the same valley, we are sure this is
the right address,
the valley of gun with treasury bills facing a depressed president shot
between choirs of Congress. Lincoln, the valley has long been named!
The equation is: wipe the smile off the face,

but the face is a photograph, a still, knows more about us than

we know,
we know,
we see,
we look at the face not from the valley of gun but from the valley of the
shadow, from throw away the key and seek the penalty,

no lock,
no key,
no murderous thought protects us from *we*, and
no easy denominations of the sick and the well.

In the valley of gun all is well, the word problem is solved: the car
    is the mayor's, silly,
he leads the parade,
he arrives in 5 minutes, the valley's a glade,

all will be well when he pulls off his mask
and you see underneath the photograph.
O now congregants who flee the scene:
watch the face tele-meme project across the terrified states
and repeat after meme,
'Lead us not into temptation.'

iii. 'Are you happy now, to unre(mem)b(e)r:
a facial erasure of the Ax Ishmæl.' —Seung-Hui Cho

Oh the happiness I could have had mingling among you hedonists. You could have been great. I could have been great. But what you did to me:

> clean the slate, brute-restraint, ravenous rape, Descendants of Satan, single second wasted, the innocent Children, band aid to patch up, wanna perpetrate endless sessions of crucifixions, 88, by destroying we create, pain you can never feel but with our hands, donation money to turn the situation, reverberate throughout.

Oh generation after generation, what I do:

> the shit you've given me, right back at you with hollow points.

An Able Physiologist 8

(The Attendees Make a Mid-Conference Social Excursion to Humber College Cemetery, Which Speaks.)

Ignored, an ignorant field arranges gravestones to slough from sight into
blankets of earth. The interred never found sense enough to mend.

Wooden crosses constructed in a hospital shop enact the process of
madness: obscure rot.

Brothers: deaf to decades of therapeutic custody,
who missed wives.

A gate, plaque and gardener.

The deep ground is bed, sky their roof.
Visitors are madhouse hours.

Keep free in me.

Subdivisions encroach our imperfect abandonment, soon to be a perfect
abandonment,

just wait.

An Able Physiologist 9

(Our Forensic Colleague Presents Her Own Case History Called 'In Thy Orisons, Ashley Smith'.)

The apples in my hand incarcerate dreams. I lived with my mother in a grim land, a place where apples appeared in the orchard perennial. I ate the fairy tale and I slept

in the pained refrain of bondage of self, in five-point restraint and spit-shield, drugs in the bore spouting sleep, drugs that praise 'You are better at rest, calm down, submit' to arms, legs, and bodies grinding my chest, pressing my thought to pulse and compressed breath, sleep

into dreams themselves restraints. No, no orchard. Just one scrub tree spitting gnarled fruit a week a year. Once in a fairy tale I was told I reached for the bough that slung low, that I shook it for a rain of projectiles. My mother hid me in this orchard because she first dreamed me there. In dreams

I want to fuck my guards, my doctors, I want to fuck the needles. I want the needles in my pouch. I lick walls to look crazy, I just like the taste. No one knows when I'll hit them in the face. As they reach for the ties I go for their eyes and smile and ask 'Do you like to watch?' I get bed-sores for punishment, the drugs knock me down like truncheons, bed-sores form the crown of the immobile high tone I've perfected accentual

and green,
with waves, the small black stem puncturing the green. With the green in my hand, I watched the mailman come for me with messages.

I wanted to give him a dream but saw him reject the gift and refuse the bough of my face. I gathered a dozen more, held them in the hem of my sundress, waited and watched as dreams became confused, they wandered into the forest

and no-intervention policies, engorged blue as per edict, the weight on my chest, the ligature on my neck, if they come in too soon they fuck me as I blind them, I am that message, o love.

Just three years ago, the Petitcodiac wondered if it could arise and go now. I walked to the river and threw dreams into its polluted breast. Moncton's grime and debris coated the green but yet kept it afloat, armouring it. I entered the water in my sundress and brought the apple to my breast, the apple dark and particulate. It tasted like walls. That month I spent in bed, with a fever no doctor could dream right. I slept with the apple core.

The centre of attention? The world of my mother is alone. 'Where is Ashley?' isn't a question. Truth in kind is not kind. Made to be entangled, blood-decorated at birth, suspect human, who'll untie me ever after, who'll kiss me alive

under the pillow, a broken pearl of dream.

Needles and cores are the same injection. The poor guards hate what I want. I never feel until I'm hated, the crazy one with the fevers and feints, don't come in too soon, it's not candy in the oven.

In church I once heard the priest talk of Saint Teresa, slings and arrows, outrageous fortune. 'In the orison of union,' says Saint Teresa, 'the soul is fully awake as regards God, but wholly asleep as regards things of this world and in respect of herself. During the short time the union lasts, she is as it were deprived of every feeling, and even if she would, she could not think of any single thing. Thus she needs to employ no artifice in order to arrest the use of her understanding: it remains so stricken with inactivity that she neither knows what she loves, nor in what manner she loves, nor what she wills. In short, she is utterly dead to the things of the world and lives solely in God … I do not even know whether in this state she has enough life left to breathe. It seems to me she has not; or at least that if she does breathe, she is unaware of it. Her intellect would fain understand something of what is going on within her, but it has so little force now that it can act in no way whatsoever. So a person who falls into a deep faint appears as if dead.' The Saint in my head, the black apple core, the priest wearing the billowing robes of Gertrude, singing off-key at an altar draped in quilted banners, the tree of life erupting in the banners, the tree of life shining in stained glass, the tree of life grows aslant the brook, the tree of life bears fruit to fall upon polluted waters. Possessed of image, I wanted to be clean but

the multifaith chaplain came and he wouldn't fuck me. I asked him to exorcise me, to fuck me. I licked the walls and showed him my tits and told him it was the same thing, right? To be clean?

I threw away

dreams and let the tree of life throw its shadow: on my face loosed of hell, to speak of horrors, the method of my face a shadow cast by the bars of this place. The tree of life, rooted in the ground, can never be free. The roots exist in the black Petitcodiac, the black roar that envelops the green, the black that nourishes the hardened boughs. I cannot see the sun move. I doubt it moves.

I am dying, crying wolf,

as

the guards are told to watch with whips and scorn. They goad me in anger, sing

Resurgo.

Was I five years old when I first heard the tidal bore? I ask guards for apples as I tie my neck. I fight them if they enter too soon. I have hours to be wrong. Guards gone, I'm rooted in a Monktown of flood plain and scrub orchard. Guards come on the shadow on my face, they come as sorrows not single spies but battalions, shove an apple in my mouth, *fucking pig.* I ate the apple long ago, the apple perennial, an apple with seeds that grew into the tree of life.

An Able Physiologist 10

(Jacques Lacan in the mirror during a variable-length
psychoanalytic session.)

The priest is the father and uses the name. The name is also the name
of my own father. The name is my name: father. There is no name
that comes before mother; but the name I know and the name I bear
comes from elsewhere, a name that never knew the game that assigns
men and women roles of love. The priest is the father and can love
only god; the priest is the father who loves the Father. My father
possessed his name. In turn, he named me. I look upon worlds
of shifting symbol and decide what names there are for emotion.
For fathers, rigor is the science of names. *Psychosis is a trial*
in rigor … I am psychotic for the sole reason that I have
always tried to be rigorous. The name on my face is for lovers to seize,
reject, or embrace. All paternity involves metaphoric substitution,
the use of names tames the complex hates we have for partial success.
The name of my name is a composite,

father,

a brand and chant that resurrects me, daily, from the dead.
The name is spoken by sons and wives but it forgets, too,
how it is bestowed. I am a father but a father like Lear who at the end
had only his own kingdom to fear, asking: *Who is it that can tell me who I am?*

An Able Physiologist II

(Dying in New York on September 12, 1977.)

The time is a summer, an autumn, a winter, a spring, another summer; here the poem ends.
Robert Lowell

The stark-rave: something of a girl in summer, encumbered with wheat-
coloured manuscripts (all love letters) and the flaxen recall
of lithium lost to time, time that's like the summer: gone,
just like the girl.

My poem about the Union: versions of self-myth.
And   O
to be a quixotic Chinook in a New York cab on the spawning instinct
to return to my ex-wife (yet a girl) and the reconciliation
that's swimming upstream: to deliquesce salt!

Summer and the wave. Summer and the grave, grace of grim
stones washed blank from salt water off the coast of Maine
and its nested coastlines of eyes.

The girl in summer turns over in her bed, her sheets lift in a wave, she's become myth. Dead men ghost the whaling stations of her sleep. I was coming to her but I died watching want drown in these seas of cosmopolitan streets that seethe past the smudged window, men and women on crosswalks marching to the orders of General Washington, who was beautiful.

Traffic lights shine on my chest pain and arrest, shine from red to green and back, Homeric myths and love transcripts exceeding my reach as messenger only. I wanted the girl in the end. Remember me that way. My tide recedes to the girl who once read a handwritten 'Man and Wife' but never agreed to the mythology, preferring love instead.

Dead men agree with the dead men of the square and common. Bronze statues honour the Union and Confederate dead, man and wife refusing either role. Dead men require hospital prophets and propitious times and the cleave of apostrophic iconography: fish and mortuarial Christ and actuarial salt and cemeterial Boston, your various religions couldn't save.

In the death-car I can't see far, just instants of hurled salt before the eyes: Lord   I prayed   in the name of freedom that is mad: the girl was and will always be a dead republic, magnolia white, dragging me home alive. She has the role of the open hand of the beautiful General shadowing the cobblestone square. Lord let me be remembered with my book in her sunbathed hand looking past what I never wrote (the Boston my heart Common). I was never there.

An Able Physiologist 12

(Darwin's Theory of Fervourism as Methodology of *The Scream*.)

From my father I inherited the seeds of madness. The angels of fear, sorrow, and death stood by my side since the day I was born.

Edvard Munch

My father, the doctor and fanatic who kept spirit ascetic: deny want until want erupts on the face, a roar of white light cast on a cortical screen, light that erodes flesh. Adapt, let bone become a want-mask. My father, the physician evangelical attended my bedside with stories about monsters, killers, and houses of screams.

I remember his story about a small boy, my age, found hanging from the rafters by a rope. The boy's father told the police that a ghost put his son there. The ghost terrified the father and son at night for nine months with threats of dangling. Each morning, the father removed ropes from the boy's neck. The magistrate sentences the father to hang. My father emulates the story-father's face: engorged eyes, translucent skin, the face that finds a dead son. 'The end. Time to sleep.
Let us pray …'

I remember my sister's face at the foot of Ekeberg. Too ill to fend for herself, Laura Catherine was admitted to the madhouse. Laura's self-portrait came through her voice: wails resounding off walls, our father dead and yet Laura wishing to return to father, father, father, home. Laura Catherine, locked in the cross of dual, disappointed wishes …

My self-portrait? Stretched to the limit, nature screaming in my blood, I first gave up hope of ever being able to love again. Never having loved before, it was easy. The sun set. The sky turned my colour, not of my face, but of its source; tongues of fire erupted above the blue-black fjord and the city.

What screams infinity and infinitely as far back as I can remember? My father with ghost stories and poverty. As far forward as I can predict, tonight, a night and beginning: my own bridging nature.

An Able Physiologist 13

(James Holmes declares that Oberon sent him to administer love-in-idleness to the patrons of the Theatre-in-the-Round in Aurora, Colorado.)

Mere mortals, I descend from the roof as a suspended fairy. You, with your arms around your lovers' necks—see the strings of my magic. Twelve of you are right asleep with my potion seeping through closed eyes. When you wake, you will love the first person you see.

I am a nerved fairy—dreams are curious upon the dead. Just now a two-troupe of rude mechanicals are at dream-end, the potion gently placed upon their sight. Just like them, I am clothed in dream-replete armour.

Quiver readied, hair reddened, I prepare for mischief. O I never knew love myself when doing the bidding of monstrous masters. I come to kill on the orders of master Oberon.

I too rest in the dream of the language, in neuronal maps of the zebra finch. Fly, russet-pated choughs! Many in sort, rising and cawing at the gun's report, sever themselves and madly sweep the sky like bats and men. Their sense weak, I lead them on in fear. O love I never expected to see you here,

> so still and now settled upon the carpeted bough of the floor.
> Twelve are down. I kill some more, heroes with the full
> onset of love-in-idleness. Fifty-four have but a partial dose,
> they seethe out, pressed close; I rub the potion upon red
> stumps and gapes.

This, I swear, Oberon made me do, on microRNA strands that drop from the sky, strings of theatre that regulate the genome post-translation, or anon, and are obscurely involved in disease.

An Able Physiologist 14

(Capone, the Neurosyphilitic, Speaks.)

How much money, where; how to be an invisible man, wrapped in bandages, all Chicago plastered in ashes. Out the window, I watch the snow. A thousand whores, or a hundred thousand—who knows who loves whom when everyone falls down dead, or, drunk, we beg to come home.

I don't want blondes, brunettes, or even the sweetest job.
You can't catch me.

Nightmare of Tommy guns exploding into the bed, men who took the Volstead road to Couderay: the road of the smuggled dead, men who profit in song. They fire into the sheets. No Chicago beat for ballistics, no Ness to lock us up, the local coroner's priced by Moran's men. To be free is to have no record, no face, no baby blues. The window's squat, square, and bullet-scared.

Take my picture—I'll pose, my forehead against the glass.

Or I'll walk up the road and find an alley to Chicago,
return to fedoras and thirsty men.

Who pays, who is paid?

Currency is good and clean and fine, I sit on stacks of bills that armour me, protection money for Snorky. Stray bullets kill kids and mothers. Husbands don't want money, so it's money and threats because money can't make people wise. Threats grease bills down throats.

Couderay is just snow and trees. No letters to this address.
I've fancied placing a dollar bill in an envelope and mailing one to Ness.
But then why not every Chicagoan, every American no less?
A dollar bill from a common crook, evading tax like nobody's business.
Money grows on trees, you stupid fucks, the fucking trees
grow because you tend the soil and you get fucking rich.
Cross me and you're dead from the pursuit of happiness.

Kneel in St. Mary's of Czestochowa to understand that I give the people what they want. We die wrapped in the wealth of not knowing how or why the end comes.

This philosopher's window in Couderay is for hiding from temptation. In a few days I'll shoot up a restaurant to remind the public the proof of their booze. But the trees here seem proof enough of another life. So why look? I look out the window and see snow rise—I hide from no one in scars. If Snorky made a snowman the boys'd laugh but if I make the weakest do it then I affirm I'm king. So go do it, you asshole fuck, go make me Frosty the Fuck Snowman. I watch you from the kitchen table in Couderay.

I'll leave Couderay Man, wrapped in syphilitic snow, before he melts.

Afterword to Conference Proceedings

(Editor's Testimony.)

> Reich Leader Bouhler and Dr. Brandt are charged with the responsibility for expanding the authority of certain physicians, to be designated by name, to the end that patients who are considered incurable according to the best available human judgment, can be granted a mercy death—from the Euthanasia Decree of Adolf Hitler of October 1939 (backdated).

I sing *Lebensunwertes Leben* to the family tune; I sing to ghosts who discern. My competence enlarged, I sing outside the gates of the *Gemeinnützige Stiftung für Heil- und Anstaltspflege.* On what basis do men judge? On what basis do men sing? I sing *Lebensunwertes Leben* as I hold my son in my arms, racked with the epileptic condition. My competence thus enlarged, I am designated by Neilson, my name, my history, my son. *Lebensunwertes Leben*—my song.

In asylum, the children are alone. The children are dead, their ashes (not their ashes) sent home with a certificate. Designated by name. With my son in my arms, the song is my diagnosis, his diagnosis, the diagnosis of *we*. His name and my name are noted in *Der Reichsausschuss zur wissenschaftlichen Erfassung von erb- und anlagebedingter schweren Leiden.*

Only on sawdust and sand can I bed, though lately my incurable competence is enlarged: I took my son to cinema showings of *The Inheritance*, *The Victim of the Past*, and *I Accuse*. All through, the boy convulsed in my arms. He was too young to know the song, but his body was yet in tune.

In Bernberg there is the song, in Brandenburg, Grafeneck, Hadamar, Hartheim, and Sonnestein; wearing a white coat I travel on a bus of the Community Patients Transport Service, my son in my arms, the seizure on his brain, the fever in my head, the song on our lips. We share the same name and without anaesthesia the needle of phenol is stuck in our hearts, my competence is enlarged, he is epileptic,

I am mentally defective,
I have no euphemism for pain,

I want none.

I am a certain physician with the responsibility of mercy and death, my son and I granted what sticks in two hearts: the human diagnosis.

Notes

This book is the partial record of a conference, 'Any Able Physiologist', held in Vienna. Because the theory of fervourism developed by Charles Darwin (1809–82) shook the world of physiology and psychiatry when originally published, the editor asked Darwin to present further thoughts about fervourism as a keynote address. The editor put out a call for papers based on Darwin's theory. A host of famous clinicians, researchers, and patients responded to the call by submitting abstracts. The best of these abstracts were selected and their authors invited to present full papers at the conference. Several responses have been collected together in this small volume but it is the editor's hope that, at a later date, the full record of the conference will be published.

(1) 'Conference Preamble: Fervourism' is adapted from *The Expression of the Emotions in Man and Animals*. London: John Murray, Albemarle Street, 1872.

(2) Phillipe Pinel in 'An Able Physiologist 1' brought a painting of his own face to the conference. This painting depicted the great nosologist's face as encircled by a manacle. When making his introductions to the audience, he exclaimed, 'To have and to hold is the problem of human life. Which is which, and which is what? I painted this myself.' Pointing his finger at the audience, he added, 'Then I painted out some words and called it *Nosographie philosophique ou La méthode de l'analyse appliquée à la médecine*.'

(3) 'An Able Physiologist 2' constitutes the lyrics Dr. Rush sang to the scientific audience. 'After much practise with the melody,' he said, 'honed when making my rounds at the Philadelphia Hospital, I hummed and muttered out the song to the general tune of the place.' Rush claims

that he stole the melody from his hospital and from folk songs current at the time and is quite angry with the obvious plagiarism of Julia Ward Howe.

(4) The epigraph from 'An Able Physiologist 3' is taken from *The Selected Writings of Benjamin Rush*, edited by Dagobert D. Runes. New York: Philosophical Library, 1947. In this presentation, Robin Pecknold (1986—) describes his own institutionalization in Dr. Rush's Pennsylvania Hospital. Pecknold is the lead singer of Seattle Band *The Fleet Foxes*. Dr. Rush (1746–1813) is considered to be the 'Father of American Psychiatry', in part because of his authorship of a seminal psychiatric textbook, *Medical Inquiries and Observations Upon Diseases of the Mind*. Philadelphia: Kimber and Richardson, 1812. This, the first psychiatry textbook published in America, went through five editions and was studied by generations of medical students. Dr. Rush also was co-signatory to the Declaration of Independence and is believed to have written a sequel to his successful psychiatric text in the few months before he died, but this sequel was never found. It is possible that Rush wrote about Pecknold in the lost text. I hope to discover this lost manuscript one day, perhaps safely stowed in some church attic, yet to be uncovered by an able antiquarian.

(5) 'An Able Physiologist 4' is the editor's translation of Emil Kræpelin's oral reading of a single entry from his dream diary *Über Sprachstörungen im Traume. Leipzig:* Verlag von Wilhelm Engelmann, 1906. Dr. Kræpelin (1856–1926) is responsible for the current classification system in psychiatry—a far more important figure than Freud (who, I must point out, histrionically refused to come to the conference once he heard the editor of this volume, me, had invited Dr. Kræpelin).

(6) 'An Able Physiologist 5' consists of two songs by Lead Belly (1888–1949) that describe his death at the hands of Irene, a woman he loved, and the aftermath of that death. The account was delivered to conference attendees in song. Though participants were invited to sample coffee and biscuits during Lead Belly's performance so as to offer a 'break' of sorts, most of those in attendance preferred to watch Lead Belly play. The phenomenon is well-described in *The Life and Legend of Leadbelly*. Charles Wolfe & Kip Lornell. New York: Da Capo Press, 1999. Wolfe and Lornell describe a typical Lead Belly performance to rich white people: 'The crowd eagerly asked for more.... Two hours after the meal was over they still lingered, draining his repertoire of Negro ballads, working songs and reels and filling his ears with applause and his battered hat with jingling coins.'

(7) 'An Able Physiologist 6' is written by C.W. Beers himself, a close friend and colleague who entrusted me to keep silent about a personal secret he could not mention in *A Mind That Found Itself*. I will keep that secret until the last, the keeping of such a great and true crime.

(8) 'An Able Physiologist 7' required strong security and closed captioning. I am rather proud of the fact that we pulled this panel discussion off. Thank you, CNN, for your generous sponsorship.

(9) 'An Able Physiologist 8' has no published text to rely upon. Cemeteries speak only to the mad. The ground left a letter near an unmarked grave which I picked up and placed in my pocket for later transcription.

(10) 'An Able Physiologist 9' is an account by Ashley Smith (1988–2007) of her witnessed suicide at the Grand Valley Institution for Women in Kitchener, Ontario. To draw her thoughts together, Smith admitted she relied upon Shakespeare's *Hamlet* and William James' *The Varieties of Religious Experience*. London & Bombay: Longmans, Green & Co., 1902.

(11) 'An Able Physiologist 10' displays the legendary jealousy of Jacques Lacan towards his intellectual colleague Michel Foucault. Lacan exploded grammar in his *The Psychoses*, especially Book 3 of *The Seminaires de Jacques Lacan*. Michel Foucault analysed power in *Madness and Civilization* and became the father of antipsychiatry. It is always good to be a father of something, and so, in terms of fatherhood, Foucault bests his compatriot. Patrimony matters to Freudians.

(12) The epigraph to the presentation by Robert Lowell (1917–1977) in 'An Able Physiologist 11' comes from his *Notebook: 1967–1968*. New York: Farrar, Straus and Giroux, 1969. It describes the plot of that book and also the plot of Lowell's presentation.

(13) 'An Able Physiologist 12' is unusual in that it is a sequel to a paper that was initially accepted for presentation ('Locked Ward Cameo: I Am Christian Munch') but the antecedent paper was lost to us because its author couldn't present the paper in person due to an attack of nerves. Christian Munch was a no-show, though his son Edvard dutifully came and added to the sum of our knowledge greatly by developing the hematological principle of a 'scream' in the blood. He apologized for his father's absence by quoting from Sue Prideaux's *Edvard Munch: Behind the Scream*. New Haven: Yale University Press, 2005: 'My father is a man

who "loved … in that intense inarticulate way of the convert who comes late to his cause, dazzled and uncomprehending." So you can see, Father can't help but come late to matters of lesser importance.'

(14) 'An Able Physiologist 13' is a midsummer night's dream of costume, war, and how a nation finds nothing new under the sun or in its cinema. James Holmes dressed in tights again to deliver his soliloquy.

(15) 'An Able Physiologist 14' is an account by Al Capone concerning his therapeutic convalescence in Couderay, Wisconsin. Before making his presentation, he insisted obscurely that his 'biographer' was wrong, that he (Capone) was in Couderay the whole three mysterious months in question of 1924, as invisible as snow. While taking questions from the audience following his presentation, Capone clarified he was referring to Laurence Bergreen's *Capone: The Man and the Era*. New York: Simon & Schuster, 1996.

(16) 'Afterword to Conference Proceedings' relies upon a particular dream of a perfect life that buried its dead. The dream occurred on a certain night in a hospital not too far from you or I, in distance or in time. This dream relies upon a frightening ghost story called *The Nazi Doctors: Medical Killing and the Psychology of Genocide* by Dr. Robert Lifton. New York: Basic Books, 2000.

OUT OF THE MOUTH OF BABES AND SUCKLINGS

BOOK THREE

HAST THOU ORDAINED STRENGTH

That which is crooked cannot be made straight:
and that which is wanting cannot be numbered.

Ecclesiastes 1:15

O Lord of the Seizure Pass

O lord this too shall pass   in the holly   the hedges   the hot poker
the closed fist   what doesn't kill me keeps me under the
horseman's cold eye and strange countenance of mind

Who conceals the writ of this place?   The hidden drama of the world
passing by   the usual advice to just let go   no   I pass

the landscape of face: imprint of seizures   sons   O lord what passes
now as the nature of grace   so close to the common and you
                    on high hosanna   of hedges holly   a hero of ache

the faces of pain neither virtuous nor true   they scream for me and they
scream for you   the last pass the first according to who   what will I
have when all this is through   bones shall   teeth shall   my
heart will not pass   O lord we stay where we are needed buried
    last

    in shallows

and thou shalt not your command   teeth for tooth   the lost for the
found   the once for the only   the before for the wake   the pass of
sceptres   robes   and consecrated space   the grave where I sit   the
scripture of my face   O lord

                                        tell Michael to pass when

the apocalypse sweeps   my lips trace epitaphs to
replace   a small hand in mine
                                                            I'll never let go   and
though you claim the shadow of the valley of graves   O
lord   I mask this estate

Fast

Only toys with wheels, good the medicine isn't any, good soft. Blankie sleep the baby monitor tonight. At the daycare Isla and Julia have eyes I close. My eyes I want, my mommy I want, mommy read me. This story this story. Writes itself mad. Mad! I mad! My medicine not good. For Halloween I pumpkin, I watch. Neighbours give you extra. Candy I love. Everyone love. Does this can I sleep? You is it better? Not to know I get bigger and bigger and then I. Big luck hardens into a bat, I see you play this truck has big. Fast wheels black sleep between seizures. Faster and faster like a little lamb from scripture black. Sheep baa baa and take. The medicine so good candy. A bat to beat advice. I cough if medicine go too fast, you can take. A toy to the daycare, a truck? Let's hug I. Want my mommy I wanted. Something different I show. Truck my friends let me show. You how to spin wheels, really really fast.

The writhe is beautiful.
I colour with green
the elevate head button.
On the hospital bed the green
from arms, the revolt of the spirit
that says let him free, the time I
held, I've carried him to altars
on television, mens are green,
he is taken, the whole world
in his hands, men die every day
from lack of what is found there, green
each time he is dying green
legs and green
arms are tired I heard: green,
a church bell on Sunday in grass,
on snow, on pavement, in car seats,
the entirely beautiful, lullaby,
don't hold me, yea though I walk
I wake and see to close my eyes
and see, I see him ruin and be
a dream. They weeble and they wobble
and they don't fall down.
When he falls:
too fast.

I not know wish. Sleep, mommy's bed. I listen for thrashing.

At night I not tired. Is this the end, the hop-sital? Have big toys they will keep you. In iso confined to bed what. That is that is truck with wheels, it big and big wheels, and go fast. My shows I watch you. Die and die again, in dreams go Big. Park don't throw sand, climb too high, share the car, we go. I like green out of your mouth. Red read me book. In the brain I park my cars, wakey-wakey mommy-daddy.

When I'm lyin in my bed at night, I don't wanna. Grow up can I? Drive car when you stop. Car as fast as I? Can to get to the hospital? Iggle Piggle has soft blankie. At show's end, Iggle Piggle falls I silly. In love, a monster eat my toes.

Into bed,
tucked up tight,
now who wants to say good night?

Lithe, sleek, the discharge clamours past
the synapse that seeks to spark a resonant
wave. Reap the curve of the scythe:
the cortex a sundowning effect,
the crescent blade cutting past what we dream
and know how to be: the waves recede to traced
shores, at length to hospital this man
was limited. If the seizure is to stop, requisite magicks
must be performed and how to dowse,
how to dowse. The stick figure is standstill
in the distance, hand frozen in a fractured
line. Where it stops, nobody knows,
the curse that takes genetics
and renders
them as fire singing old
connections.
Burnt wiser and fragile,

worse transcriptions
of a dream
tired of singleness.

I slow the truck to get load, a rock tree and juice. I slow to stop. Legs no work for playplace. I slow to warm up. I slow like doctor and her. I slow listen to you. Count hide in closet and slow! Trucks go fast and then slow and I park them, trucks, I give slow.

Brittle bank, slippery slope, the reach and curse
of watching back at pinpoint lights, little fires,
encampments that renege on promise except to strike
in sneak attack and the stroke sets in motion
the prime mover and the body in motion stays in motion

and by what graven image shall we know
the thoughtful second coming of demon casting,
the holding hands of shaking hands of conduction,
of a conductor's
hands setting astray symphonies
in order, the cellular song's hundred million
membranous throats clucking in choked unison, an inheritance!

Strobe, cast, enisled, to falter, to father,
to settle, to stop revealing.

On windows, see yellow white. See trees frozen. Night night says Mr. Crow, are you tickly on your toe? I hold car. Then drop car, mommy find. I hold mommy next. To me snow on face. Mommy white, the light on and not should be. Sing a song of sixpence sing. For our supper sing. In heavenly choirs sing song. In circle: *tidy up time, tidy up time, toys away, toys away*. Hop-sital far. Away they have toys there? Big toys me see the mens? And rooms that go up and down and up? I push button? And mommy come too?

Look out the door. You put your. The more we get together, the happier my friends and your friends will please shine down on the trees, the breeze, the train tracks, scraped knees, the music, the view. Either you get it first or it will get you.

On the road out of Guelph. Black. In the back,
he's belted in the car seat, choked, rigid, then slack.
You sit with him, sing 'Wheels on the Bus'.
The snow comes down. What is it with us?
That pain unites? Rearview mirror:
lights and faces, in love. I want to stop the car,
walk off into the forest, and come out starving, pure,
with a cure. But the thought doesn't last. I drive
knowing that I took my chance. I have nothing else.
And so we go to another hopeless wilderness.
I hate this sound: lungs on a tether. Stopcock tongue.
The cabin light on in case he goes blue.
Where do we find our saviour? Is he two,
capable of visions, of my looking at you
when all the pediatric neurologists are asleep
and seeing the manger light seep
into your cast-out eyes? Do not look at me! And in his stupor know
just what's needed? The wilderness arrives,
or we to it. Give me prophecy. He is alive.

I lie on pyre. Carried up. And over I stretch, back from bent. Of lamb in field with no. Predating threat: as if me might die. Pain writ upon the body, a shake-pain. Entered a skin, choose to fall. Then tide rushes in, the air. Expands to meet the size. Of its container, the heart returns. To a rate of earth. Whoso list sithens in a net I seek to hold. The wind and wind seeks itself and whoso holds the list. Whoso holds the right to list and I list to earth. Fainting I follow list to dreams and list to breathe, afterward. *Noli me tangere*, kindly ones: wild for to hold, though I seem tame. Pyre-burn.

The Barn

Emblem: we spent an automatism, the sway-backed Moro response
reflecting a Landau reaction, patching rotten insides with deviations
from this rule.

Waste from the modes of stimulation; the differential fixation a hazard
until we laid the lalling stage so that a normal person as abstraction could
walk it; and we were a kind of crossmodal,

which parents come to understand. The day idioglossing us over, except
when Lennox Gastaut's up on the scaffold, making repair after repair to
form the multiplex of Friedreich. Crows, living

in the opisthotonic, hands pronated as hammers, redolent with their
Lafora-type shit, in the barn-shade for quick snorts and AED
availability. If asked, violaceous faces would complain of spike-and-wave
wages and work harder if my father was found.

Sometimes the prognosis is *bad*. The sun would heat the hyperexcitable
tin and burn though the work gloves. With panoramic vision, a young
woman *jamais entendu*, I thought

of each time I carried a piece of tin up the *grand petit absence*, just fifteen,
interictal on the wood underneath, battle hymns of the benign rolandic,
places where

it was distinguishable from *premonition* if fire or lightning had hit. We
papered it over. A jacksonian trick for the men to work past a certain
drink

and I remember looking at the old barn, house of vibratory quality: hay
and a beaten-down epileptic cry that grew monstrous in the year,

at three in the afternoon, no men around, a wife in fencer's posture soon
to be cut and the gleaming parachute reaction, a drop attack.

Out of the mouth of babes and sucklings hast thou ordained strength

In the end, the father knew something would happen. He knew he'd discover no pearly gate[1], no flourish of an angel on high, no heavenly hosanna[2] ushering his son in or through. He knew there would be the Four Horsemen[3] and the liturgy of *Why hast thou forsaken me.*[4]

---

1. The insipid idea of the pearly gate takes its origin from Revelations; it is of some doubt whether Saint Peter actually is the guardian who decides upon admittance. The father never liked this idea, for heaven shouldn't be opulent in a crass, corporeal way. If he did meet Peter, he'd ask Peter if he was still the rock of the church, or if he was instead the bauble. He'd then ask for Peter's job.
2. Hosanna originates from a Hebrew word that means 'Save, I pray.' This is a particularly rich word in that one sees that the saving is meant to come first and the praying comes after; though one could make a case that the former is conditional or dependent upon the latter. In the Bible the phrase is *Hosanna! Blessed is the one who comes in the name of the Lord*. The trouble with hosanna is that one never really knows who is coming or when, or if the one who comes is truly blessed. The child wondered about names most of all.
3. The sexiest of the four horsemen is Conquest, though the other three bear mentioning: War, Famine, and Death. The father always felt that the Horsemen are part of an apocalyptic wet dream meant to keep the plebs in line; L. Ron Hubbard merely updated Revelations with his *Dianetics*, focusing on End Times to keep human minds perpetually in the speculative, and therefore in line. White, red, black, and a pale horse: the father always felt the variety a mistake, for terror is about visual homogeneity. All the horses should be the same color. But the subsequent torture should be individualized.
4. This bit of verbatim oratory struck the father as calculated, as was everything Christ said; a little doubt and weakness to make Christ just like us! Yet he

He envisioned a shimmering, titanic, blood-encrusted cross. If an inscription appeared above his son's head, some pithy statement meant to echo through the ages in which he and his wife were still alive, before the horsemen stole into his barn, it would be: COXCOMB[5].

What would his son's facial expression be? Would the boy look as if he were burning in perpetual fire, an agonal agony, the sympathy a prescription for lighter judgment, for alms[6] offered by intimates and

---

believed Christ more when Christ was reported to say, shortly before he died, after being on the cross for a few days, 'I thirst.'

5. 'Coxcomb' is one of the first words spoken by the fool in *King Lear*. The fool is an early instance in English Literature of ominous nonsense verse, a gauntlet taken up memorably by Charles Dodgson in the 19th century. The coxcomb in this instance (the noun can pertain to many other things, including a mountain range, a moth, a flourish on a gallinaceous bird, or a kind of edible plant) refers to a peaked jester's cap. The reference to King Lear is apt in that, shortly after trying to give Kent his coxcomb, the jester and the King enter into a discussion in which the King eventually repeats, 'Nothing can be made out of nothing.'
6. Coming from the Latin 'eleemosyna', the idea of making an offering to Christ to the church directly and also to the poor through charitable work is called 'alms'. Sadly, the Greek meaning of the word is 'compassion'. The most beautiful biblical appearance of the word comes in Luke 11:41: *But rather give alms of such things as ye have; and, behold, all things are clean unto you.*

passersby? Judge not lest ye be judged?[7] Let he who is without sin adopt the child's face?[8]

The father hoped his son wouldn't adopt the face of a god, an only begotten son, for the representations of Christ from antiquity were the paintings and sculptings of paparazzi; iconography became debased thousands of years ago. Who can know how a

---

7. This passage is an oft cited snippet of scripture, but it is less popularly known than what comes immediately after from the Gospel of Matthew (7:6): *Give not that which is holy unto the dogs, neither cast ye your pearls before swine, lest they trample them under their feet, and turn again and rend you.* Swine and pearls: all of life. Pearls are the ornamentation that permits admittance to heaven; but they are also the loves and hopes and pretty things that will be the end of us all. The Bible is so confusing.
8. The story is well known: Pharisees tried to trick Jesus into a biblical meltdown, a contradiction of commandment. An adulterous woman is brought before him; the Pharisees wish for Jesus to condemn her, but Jesus does not. Curiously, he draws in the sand with a stick until they force him to speak. A whole Christian industry has sprung up about what Jesus might have done with the stick, if he wrote parables or drew stick figures. The more interesting thing was that Jesus saved his most devastating comment for the woman when she was alone with him after the Pharisees fled Jesus for fear of their own sins being exposed. Jesus identified with the woman more than any other sinner he ever came in contact with when he said, *Woman, where are thine accusers? Hath no man condemned thee?* It was, of course, Jesus who was on trial. He was breaking the fourth wall, so to speak. It's not wise to be left alone with an adulterer …

temporarily condemned god felt inside? Who can see truth in any face?[9] There is nothing new under the sun.[10] The son would have to take his scaffolded place, like everyone. He'd bleed, suffer, and if anyone took notice, if his death meant more than a family drama, if it made an imprint like cloths applied to the face of an icon, Christ's face transferred down centuries, perfectly preserved, perfectly inscrutable.

---

9. One can't trust any picture of the Four Horsemen because they've never been actually seen by anyone; they are figments of a god's imagination. In antiquity, artists stuck to wooden representations of men on horses, but it's become a grotesque cottage industry over the years. As for Christ, the father always liked images depicting Christ playing against type: a serene Christ throwing moneychangers out of the temple, an angry Christ getting his feet washed by Mary Magdalene, a smirking Christ confronting Thomas, a lustful Christ sanctioning Judas' betrayal, a Christ looking heavenward not in the extremity of patience, of the eye roll of 'They know not what they do', but as in acknowledgement that there is nothing up there.
10. The father loved the idea that nothing was new, also the idea that nothing came from nothing; but he hated a famous line that came just a few beats later than the sun wisdom as it appears in Ecclesiastes, the same line that serves as the satanic epigraph to this section of this book.

See the Marquee

The most characteristic of all the elements
of the conversion crisis … is the ecstasy of happiness produced.
William James

I said, don't let him die, and I, I.
I will. I will change and become like the sky:
open, prismatic, where thunder and white
border incredible blue. I'll hold him and know
that I owe you. Belief is to understand
the recast plea: me, me, old family trees,
church keys, locks, fever debris.
You gave him reprieve, he stopped falling free.

What ecstasy this? I am left with *I,* a copy of *me*,
I sit in the churches and see the marquee:
a sick bleeding son, the revenant trustee.
I hold him now. Glory to God in the highest
and peace to his people on earth.
I keep the bargain like faith keeps me: angry,
small, held inside fathomless walls,
supreme sky that widens past the human gift:
give away, take away, what we want, this.

Every Age, the Erinyes

Wrested angels, choked throats: what spins
a scattered cosmology upon no sight we see:
there is nothing.

In the hospital are armaments, blast zones,
and roving fronts. But then backward angels
appear on lips, dangle from necks, look in one-way windows.
Pins and needles, dancing on the heads of pins, injected in needles.
And who could speak to true fury that lifts one child
in the minutes he doesn't know are left?

Furies waste angels. Furies blaze black and red,
incite retreats. Angels are for intercessions
but furies are for the taking, the taking of us.

I carry my son.

He shakes with fury.

The false oath is: *Can any hide himself in secret places that I shall not see him?*

The One True Cry

I've watched you die, and die again, in dreams.
My son, they say in dreams we meet.
That promise met, and one cry. I rhyme in dreams

meant not for me. But not you either! The seams
are sweet excite, the clench of arm, Humpty's empty seat.
I've watched you die, and die again, in dreams.

Humpty on the balancing beam, a father's eyegleam,
the king's horses and the king's men lofty and great.
That promise met, and one cry. I rhyme in dreams.

I too have a quiver in the brain, a vault of arrows, a stream
of electrons that circle and hurtle and make me complete.
I've watched you die, and die again, in dreams.

Targets fall like you fall, another target hit. Targets teem
but the arrows are hail, are sin-throw-the-first-stone, are sleet.
That promise met, and one cry. I rhyme in dreams.

Dreams come true for fools, madmen, kings. The truth is dreams.
Horses pull cracked targets. At night, everyone sleeps.
I've watched you die, and die again, in dreams.
That promise met, and one cry. I rhyme in dreams.

Glossolalias

1. *The Complete Works of Milton Acorn* (finished).
2. *The Complete Works of Wayne Clifford* (unfinished).
3. Davenport, Andrew. *In the Night Garden.* BBC Television.
4. *The Complete Works of Fervourist Marc di Saverio* (unfinished).
5. Dowbiggin, Ian. *The Quest for Mental Health: A Tale of Science, Medicine, Scandal, Sorrow, and Mass Society.* Cambridge: Cambridge University Press, 2011.
6. *The Complete Works of Jim Johnstone* (unfinished).
7. Lewis, C.S. *The Problem of Pain.* New York: HarperCollins, 2006.
8. Raffi. *Singable Songs for the Very Young.* Universal Music Group, 1976.
9. Ropper, Allan, and Martin Samuels. *Adams and Victor's Principles of Neurology*, 9th ed. New York: McGraw-Hill Professional, 2009.
10. *The Complete Works of Sir Thomas Wyatt* (finished).
11. Whybrow, Ian. *The Tickle Book.* New York: Macmillan Children's, 2000.
12. The King James Bible (1769 version).

Acknowledgements

Magazines:

'The Barn', published in *Arc Magazine*.

'No Sum', 'Facial Structure', 'Facies Leonina', 'Elegy Skyward' and 'Half-true incarnations of an about-face', in *The Antigonish Review*.

'Out of the mouth of babes and sucklings hast thou ordained strength', in *BlazeVOX*.

'St. Vitus' Dance', in *Canadian Medical Association Journal*.

'The Pain Face', in *Canadian Notes and Queries*.

'The Lake of Fire' and 'In the tongue of schizophasics ...', in *CV2*.

'Fast', in *The Dalhousie Review*.

'Phillipe Pinel and the Wisdom of the Clinical' and 'The Lost Writings of Clifford Whittingham Beers', in *Descant*.

'St. Anthony's Fire', in *The Fiddlehead*.

'An Able Physiologist 3: Robin Pecknold Descends the Steps of Pennsylvania Hospital in 1786', in *The Literary Review of Canada*.

'Dying in New York on September 12, 1977', in *The Malahat Review*.

'Reaching the Palace' and 'Action Potential', in *Pain and Research Management*.

'General Preamble', in *The Puritan*.

'O Lord of the Seizure Pass' and 'Face-Shaver', in *This Magazine*.

'An Able Physiologist 5' and 'An Able Physiologist 9', in *The Winnipeg Review*.

Anthologies, Chapbooks and Broadsides:

'On the Road Out of Guelph', published in *2011 Montreal Poetry Prize Longlist Anthology*.

‘Out of the mouth’, published by the Hellbox Press in 2014 in a limited edition letterpress chapbook.

‘Able Physiologists Discuss Grief Musculatures’, published in 2014 in a limited edition chapbook by Jackpine Press.

‘On Shaving Off His Face’, published by the Alfred Gustav Press in 2014 in a limited edition chapbook.

Awards:

‘The Barn’, 2013 Poem of the Year Award, *Arc Magazine*.

‘St. Anthony’s Fire’, 2012 Silver, Poetry Category, National Magazine Awards.

Shane Neilson is a family physician who published his first trade book of poems in 2009. In 2010 the Porcupine's Quill published *Complete Physical*. In addition to several more collections of poetry, Neilson has published in the genre of memoir, short fiction, biography and literary criticism, and his work has been widely anthologized in poetry, nonfiction and medical journals. In his medical doctor and writing practices, he focuses on mental illness, pain and disability. He acts as editor for Victoria, B.C. publisher Frog Hollow Press. Though he lives in Oakville, Ontario, all of his work is rooted in rural New Brunswick.